MOTO

C000224488

BASS CLASSICS

Music transcriptions by Steve Gorenberg

ISBN 0-7935-8837-5

7777 W. BLUEMOUND RD. P.O. BOX 13819 MILWAUKEE, WI 53213

Visit Hal Leonard Online at
www.halleonard.com

MOTOWN BASS CLASSICS

CONTENTS

Ain't No Mountain High Enough

Words and Music by Nickolas Ashford and Valerie Simpson

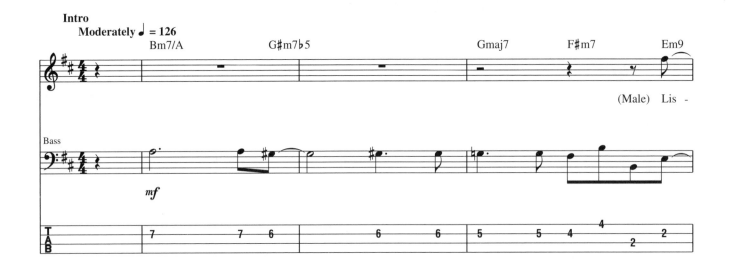

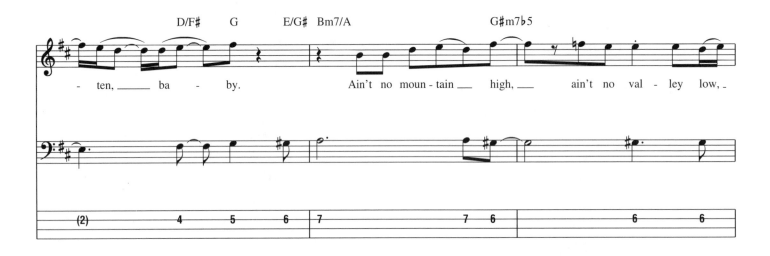

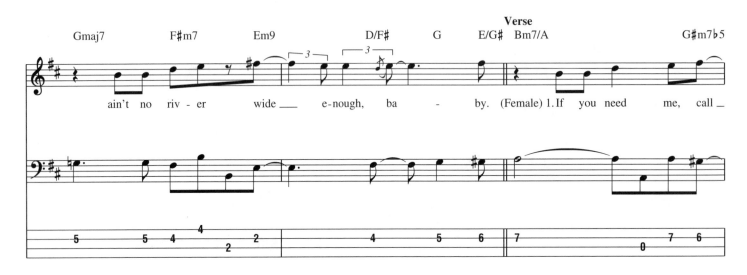

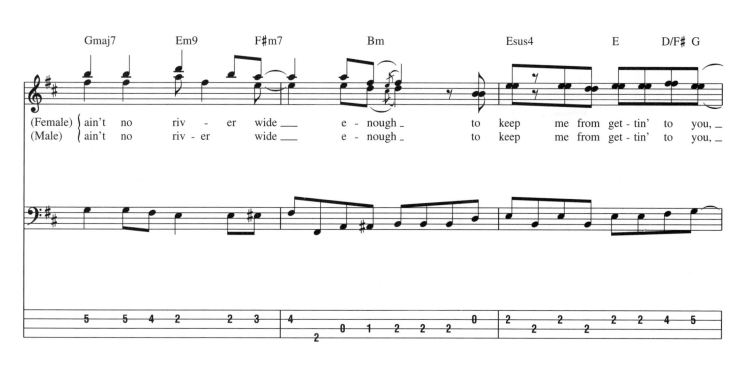

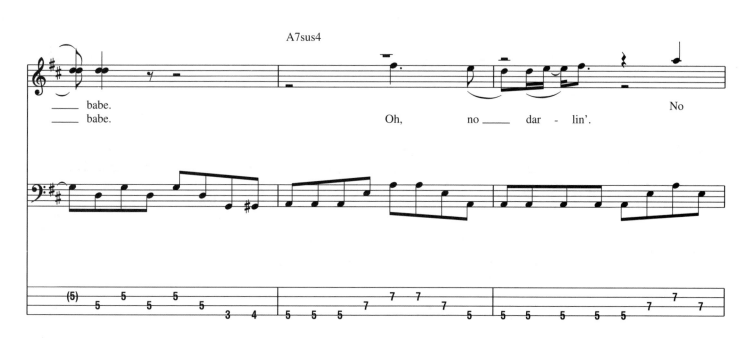

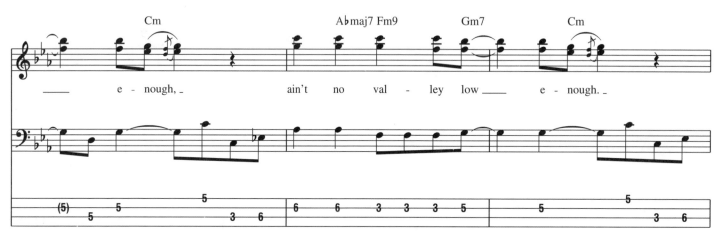

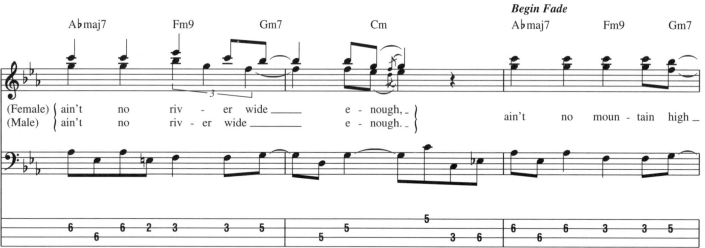

Ain't Nothing Like the Real Thing

Words and Music by Nickolas Ashford and Valerie Simpson

14

Ain't Too Proud to Beg

Words and Music by Edward Holland and Norman Whitfield

Additional Lyrics

2. Now, I've heard a cryin' man is half a man,
   With no sense of pride.
   But if I have to cry to keep you, I don't mind weepin'
   If it'll keep you by my side.

3. If I have to sleep on your doorstep all night and day
   Just to keep you from walking away.
   Let your friends laugh, even this I can stand,
   'Cause I wanna keep you any way I can.

4. Now I've got a love so deep in the pit of my heart,
   And each day it grows more and more.
   I'm not ashamed to call and plead to you, baby,
   If pleading keeps you from walking out that door.

Baby Love

Words and Music by Brian Holland, Edward Holland and Lamont Dozier

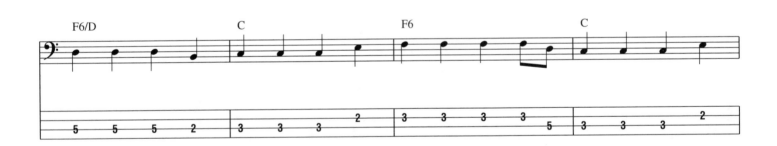

Additional Lyrics

2. 'Cause baby love, my baby love,
   Been missin' ya, miss kissin' ya.
   Instead of breaking up,
   Let's do some kissin' and makin' up.
   Don't throw our love away.
   In my arms, why don't ya stay?

3. Baby love, my baby love,
   Why must we separate, my love?
   All of my whole life through,
   I never loved no one but you.
   Why ya do me like you do?
   If get this need.

Dancing in the Street

Words and Music by Marvin Gaye, Ivy Hunter and William Stevenson

For Once in My Life

Words by Ronald Miller
Music by Orlando Murden

Get Ready

Words and Music by William "Smokey" Robinson

fe fi _____ fo _____ fum, _____
fid - dle - e - dee, fid - dle - e - dum. _____
twee - dle - e - dee, twee - dle - e - dum. _____
look out, ba - by, 'cause

Chorus

here I come. _
(Ah, _____

And I'm bring - in' you a love that's true, _ so get
get

read - y, so get read - y. _____
read - y, get read - y. _____
I'm gon - na try to make ya
Ah, _____

love me too, _ so get read - y, so get read - y. Here I come. _
_ yeah, _ get read - y, get read - y.
Get read - y, 'cause

35

I Can't Help Myself
(Sugar Pie, Honey Bunch)

Words and Music by Brian Holland, Lamont Dozier and Edward Holland

I Heard It Through the Grapevine

Words and Music by Norman J. Whitfield and Barrett Strong

Interlude

3. Peo - ple say be - lieve half _____ of what you see, _____ son, and none _
(Do, _____ do, do. _____

_____ of what you hear. _____ But I can't help _____ be - ing con - fused. _
Ooh. _____ Do, _____ do, do. _____

_____ If it's true, _____ please tell me dear. _____ Do you plan _
Ooh. _____

I Just Want to Celebrate

Words and Music by Nick Zesses and Dino Fekaris

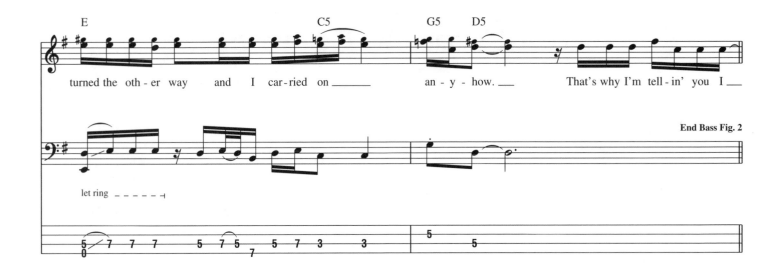

turned the oth-er way and I car-ried on _____ an-y-how. ___ That's why I'm tell-in' you I ___

End Bass Fig. 2

let ring _ _ _ _ _

Chorus

___ just wan-na cel-e-brate, yeah yeah, _ a-noth-er day of liv-in'. Yeah, _____

Bass Fig. 3

End Bass Fig. 3

Bass: w/ Bass Fig. 1
N.C.(D7)

I just want _ to cel - e-brate ___ a-noth-er day _ of life. _____

Verse

Bass: w/ Bass Fig. 2
N.C.(N7)

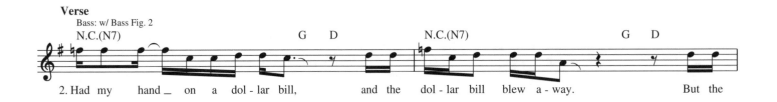

2. Had my hand _ on a dol-lar bill, and the dol-lar bill blew a-way. But the

sun is shine-in' down _ on me, _ and it's here to stay. That's why I'm tell-in' you I ___
(Here to stay. _____)

Chorus

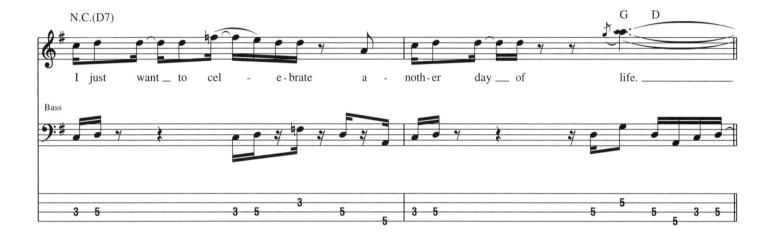

Bridge

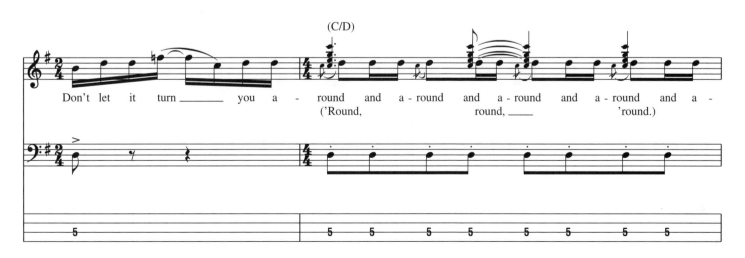

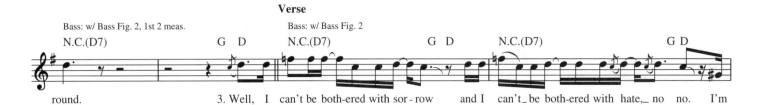

Verse

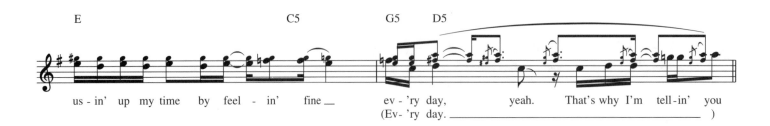

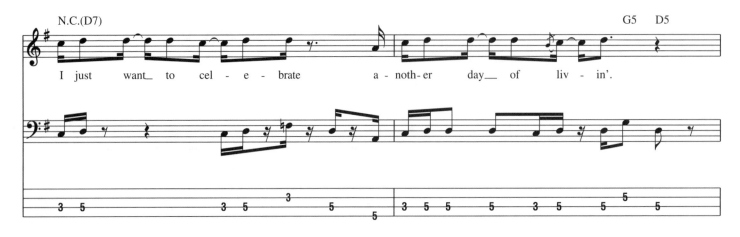

A Tempo

Outro

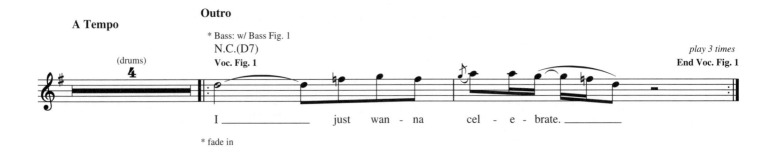

I _____ just wan - na cel - e - brate. _____

I Second That Emotion

Words and Music by William "Smokey" Robinson and Alfred Cleveland

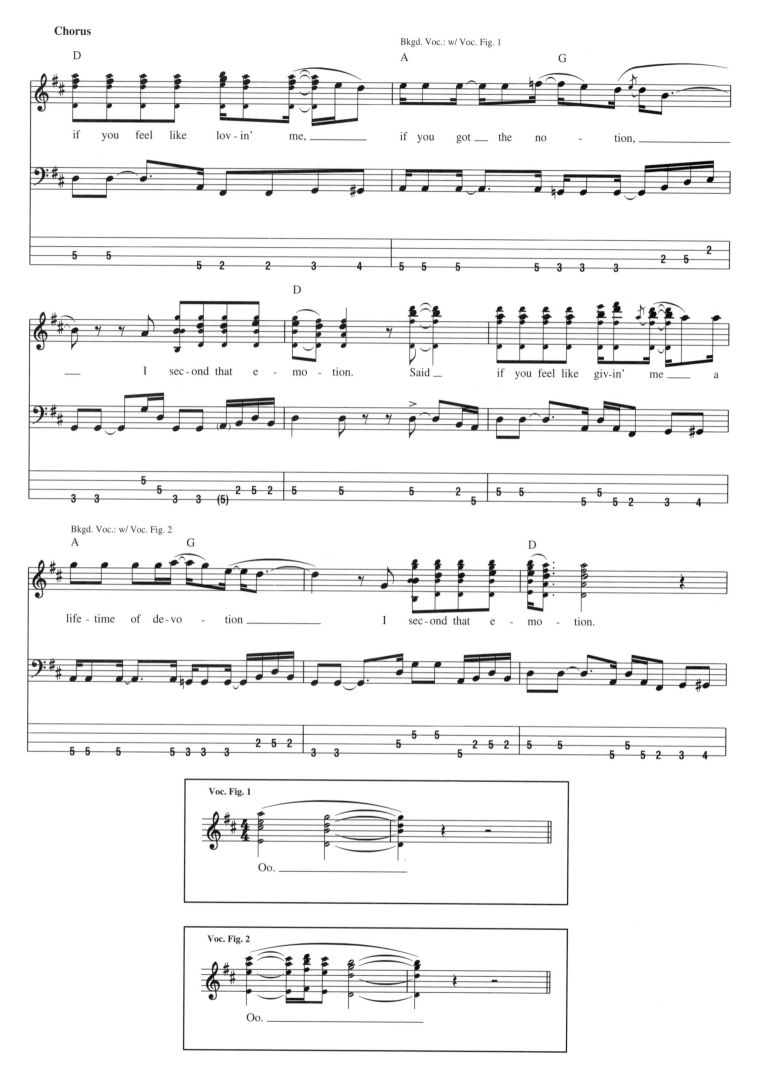

Verse

Bkgd. Voc.: w/ Voc. Fig. 3

Oh. May - be you think that love would tie you down ___ and

you don't have ___ the time ___ to hang a - round. ___ Or

Bkgd. Voc.: w/ Voc. Fig. 3

may - be you think that love ___ were made for fools. _____ And

so it makes ___ you wise ___ to break the rules. ___ Oh, ___ lit - tle girl then

Voc. Fig. 3

Oo. Doo, doo, doo, doo, doo. _____

It's the Same Old Song

Words and Music by Edward Holland, Lamont Dozier and Brian Holland

Additional Lyrics

2. Sentimental fool am I,
 To hear an old love song and wanna cry.
 But the melody keeps haunting me
 Reminding me how in love we used to be.
 Keep hearing the part that used to touch our heart,
 Saying, "Together forever, breaking up never."

3. Precious memories keep lingering on,
 Every time I hear our favorite song.
 Now you're gone, left this emptiness.
 I only reminisce, the happiness we spent.
 We used to dance to the music,
 Make romance to the music.

My Girl

Words and Music by William "Smokey" Robinson and Ronald White

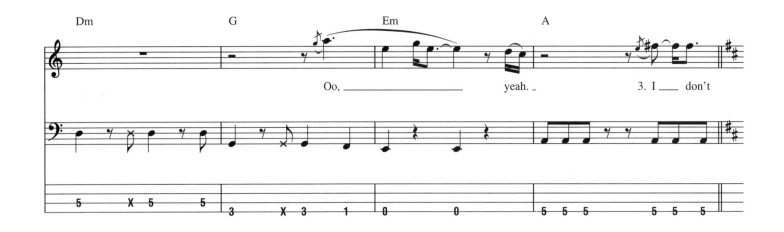

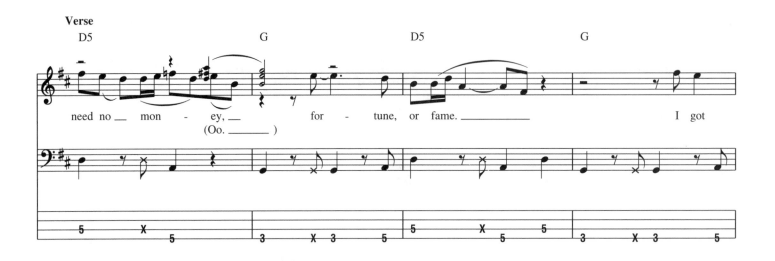

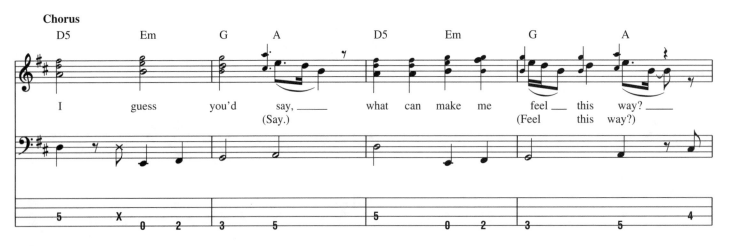

My girl, _____ talk-in' 'bout ___ my ___ girl. _____
(My girl, _____) talk-in' 'bout. ___) (My girl. Talk-in bout
(My girl.)

Outro

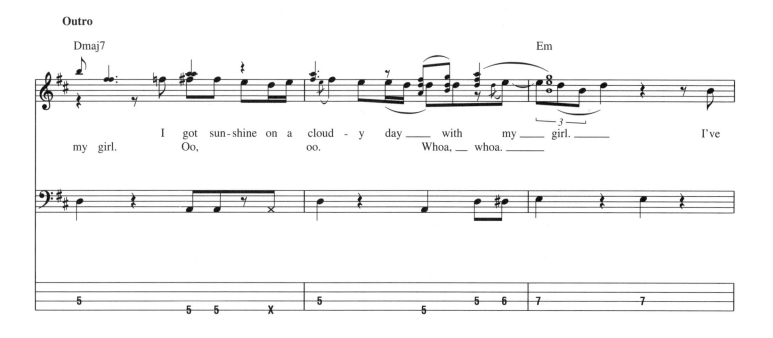

I got sun-shine on a cloud - y day ___ with ___ my ___ girl. _____ I've
my girl. Oo, oo. Whoa, ___ whoa. _____

Begin Fade   *Fade Out*

e - ven got the month ___ of May ___ with ___ my girl. _____ Talk - in' 'bout. ___
A - bout, talk - in' 'bout my girl, _____ my girl. Whoa. _____)

67

My Guy

Words and Music by William "Smokey" Robinson

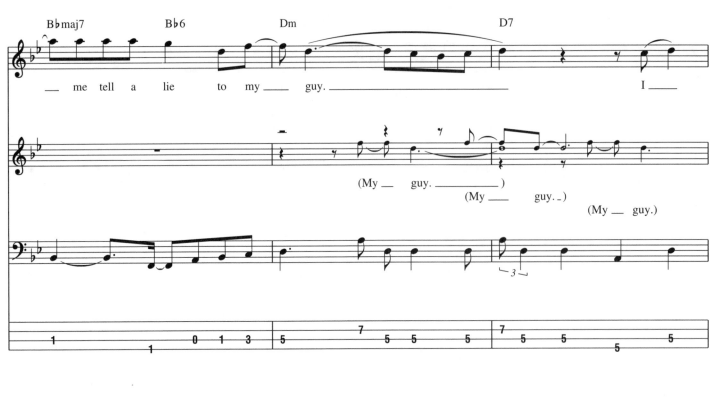

me tell a lie to my ___ guy. ___ I ___

(My ___ guy. ___)

(My ___ guy. ___)

(My ___ guy.)

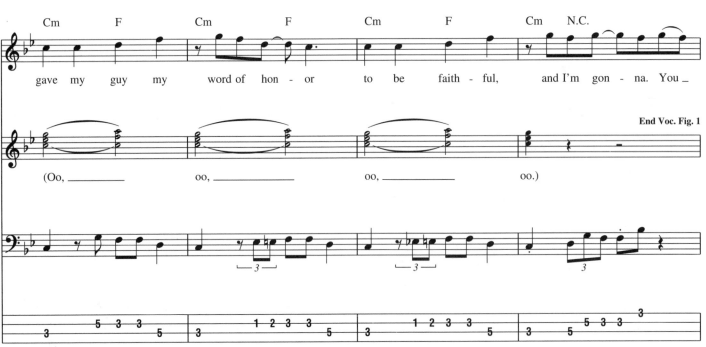

gave my guy my word of hon - or to be faith - ful, and I'm gon - na. You ___

(Oo, _____ oo, _____ oo, _____ oo.)

End Voc. Fig. 1

best be be-liev-ing I won't ___ be de-ceiv-ing my ___ guy. ___ As a

Bridge

mat-ter of o-pin-ion, I think he's tops. _ My o-pin-ion is he's the cream of the crop. As a

(Oo, _ oo, _ oo, _ oo.

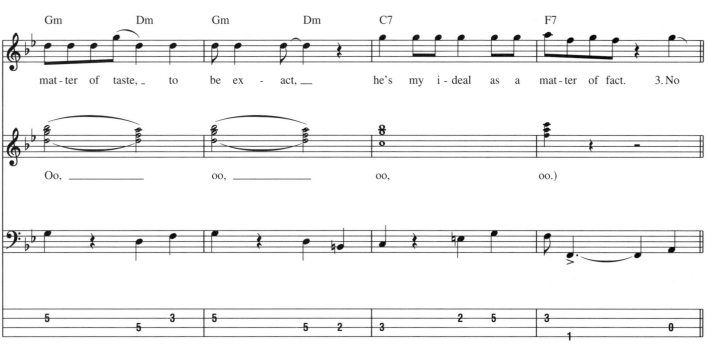

mat-ter of taste, _ to be ex - act, _ he's my i-deal as a mat-ter of fact. 3. No

Oo, _ oo, _ oo, _ oo.)

Verse

Bkgd. Voc.: w/ Voc. Fig. 1

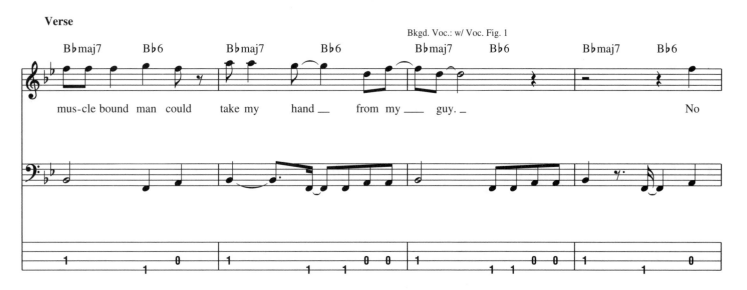

mus-cle bound man could take my hand _ from my _ guy. _ No

74

What's Going On

Words and Music by Marvin Gaye, Al Cleveland and Renaldo Benson

F♯m7/B
B7(add13)
to bring some un - der - stand-ing here to - day, oh, oh.
Bring some, stand-ing here to - day.
Pre-Chorus
F♯m7
F♯m7/B
F♯m7
Pick-et lines and pick-et signs don't pun - ish me with bru -
(Broth - er, broth - er, broth - er,
F♯m7/B
F♯m7
F♯m7/B
tal - i - ty. Come on talk to me, so you can see, ah, what's
broth - er, broth - er, broth-er.)
Chorus
Emaj7
C♯m7
go - ing on, yeah, what's go - ing on, tell me what's
(What's go - ing on, what's go - ing on,

Reach Out, I'll Be There

Words and Music by Brian Holland, Lamont Dozier and Edward Holland

Additional Lyrics

2. When you feel lost and about to give up,
   'Cause your best just ain't good enough.
   And you feel the world has grown cold,
   And you're drifting all on your own.
   And you need a hand to hold.
   Darlin', hello girl, reach out for me.
   Reach out for me.
   I'll be there to love and comfort you.
   And I'll be there to cherish and care for you...

3. I can the way you hang your head,
   You're without love now, now you're afraid.
   And through your tears you'll look around,
   But there's no piece of mind to be found.
   I know what you're thinkin': You're a loner, no love of your own.
   But darling, come on girl, reach out for me.
   Reach out. Just look over your shoulder.
   I'll be there to give you all the love you need.
   And I'll be there, you can always depend on me.

Shot Gun

Words and Music Autry DeWalt

Stop! In the Name of Love

Words and Music by Lamont Dozier, Brian Holland and Edward Holland

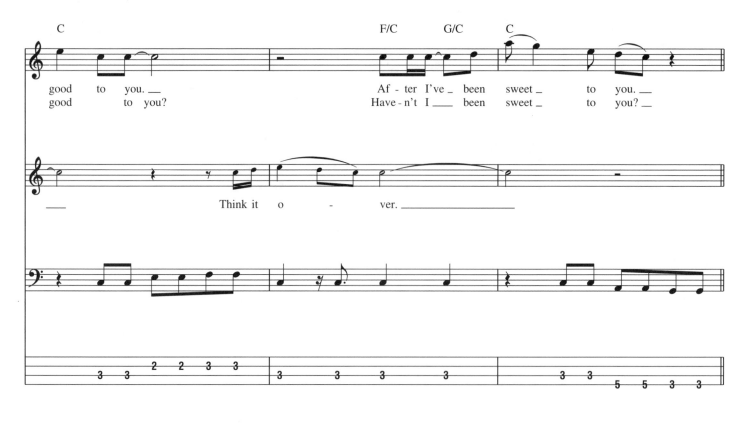

good to you. ___ After I've been sweet ___ to you. ___
good to you? Have-n't I ___ been sweet ___ to you? ___

___ Think it o - ver. ___

Chorus
w/ Lead Voc. ad lib., 3rd time

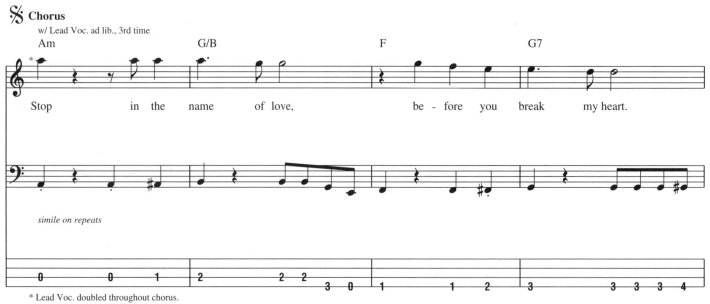

Stop in the name of love, be - fore you break my heart.

simile on repeats

* Lead Voc. doubled throughout chorus.

To Coda

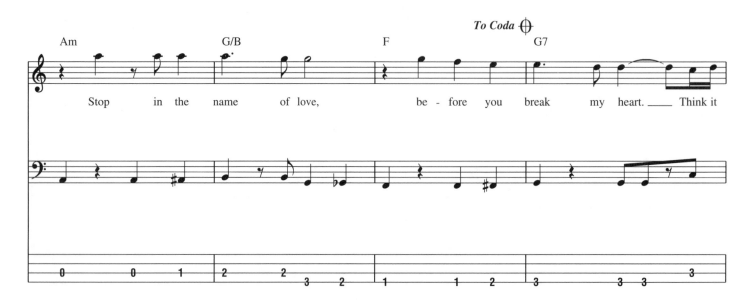

Stop in the name of love, be - fore you break my heart. ___ Think it

Where Did Our Love Go

Words and Music by Brian Holland, Lamont Dozier and Edward Holland

You Can't Hurry Love

Words and Music by Edward Holland, Lamont Dozier and Brian Holland

101

You Keep Me Hangin' On

Words and Music by Edward Holland, Lamont Dozier and Brian Holland

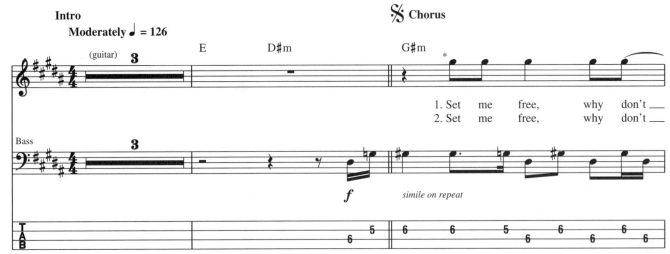

* Two lead voc. arr. for one throughout, except where otherwise indicated.

Bass Notation Legend

Bass music can be notated two different ways: on a *musical staff*, and in *tablature*.

THE MUSICAL STAFF shows pitches and rhythms and is divided by bar lines into measures. Pitches are named after the first seven letters of the alphabet.

TABLATURE graphically represents the bass fingerboard. Each horizontal line represents a string, and each number represents a fret.

Notes:

Strings:

3rd string, open   2nd string, 2nd fret   1st & 2nd strings open, played together

HAMMER-ON: Strike the first (lower) note with one finger, then sound the higher note (on the same string) with another finger by fretting it without picking.

PULL-OFF: Place both fingers on the notes to be sounded. Strike the first note and without picking, pull the finger off to sound the second (lower) note.

LEGATO SLIDE: Strike the first note and then slide the same fret-hand finger up or down to the second note. The second note is not struck.

SHIFT SLIDE: Same as legato slide, except the second note is struck.

TRILL: Very rapidly alternate between the notes indicated by continuously hammering on and pulling off.

TREMOLO PICKING: The note is picked as rapidly and continuously as possible.

VIBRATO: The string is vibrated by rapidly bending and releasing the note with the fretting hand.

SHAKE: Using one finger, rapidly alternate between two notes on one string by sliding either a half-step above or below.

NATURAL HARMONIC: Strike the note while the fret hand lightly touches the string directly over the fret indicated.

MUFFLED STRINGS: A percussive sound is produced by laying the fret hand across the string(s) without depressing them and striking them with the pick hand.

BEND: Strike the note and bend up the interval shown.

BEND AND RELEASE: Strike the note and bend up as indicated, then release back to the original note. Only the first note is struck.

RIGHT-HAND TAP: Hammer ("tap") the fret indicated with the "pick-hand" index or middle finger and pull off to the note fretted by the fret hand.

LEFT-HAND TAP: Hammer ("tap") the fret indicated with the "fret-hand" index or middle finger.

SLAP: Strike ("slap") string with right-hand thumb.

POP: Snap ("pop") string with right-hand index or middle finger.

Additional Musical Definitions

 (accent) • Accentuate note (play it louder)

 (accent) • Accentuate note with great intensity

 (staccato) • Play the note short

⊓ • Downstroke

⋁ • Upstroke

D.S. al Coda • Go back to the sign (𝄋), then play until the measure marked "***To Coda***," then skip to the section labelled "***Coda***."

D.C. al Fine • Go back to the beginning of the song and play until the measure marked "***Fine***" (end).

Bass Fig. • Label used to recall a recurring pattern.

Fill • Label used to identify a brief pattern which is to be inserted into the arrangement.

tacet • Instrument is silent (drops out).

• Repeat measures between signs.

• When a repeated section has different endings, play the first ending only the first time and the second ending only the second time.

NOTE: Tablature numbers in parentheses mean:
1. The note is being sustained over a system (note in standard notation is tied), or
2. The note is sustained, but a new articulation (such as a hammer-on, pull-off, slide or vibrato begins, or
3. The note is a barely audible "ghost" note (note in standard notation is also in parentheses).

BASS RECORDED VERSIONS

Recorded Versions for Bass Guitar are straight off-the-record transcriptions done expressly for bass guitar. This series features the best in bass licks from the classics to contemporary superstars. Also available are Recorded Versions for Guitar, Easy Recorded Versions and Drum Recorded Versions. Every book includes notes and tab.

Beatles Bass Book
00660103 / $14.95

Best Bass Rock Hits
00694803 / $12.95

Black Sabbath – We Sold Our Soul For Rock 'N' Roll
00660116 / $14.95

The Best Of Eric Clapton
00660187 / $14.95

Stuart Hamm Bass Book
00694823 / $19.95

The Buddy Holly Bass Book
00660132 / $12.95

Best Of Kiss
00690080 / $19.95

Lynyrd Skynyrd Bass Book
00660121 / $14.95

Michael Manring – Thonk
00694924 / $22.95

Alanis Morisette – Jagged Little Pill
00120113 / $14.95

Nirvana Bass Collection
00690066 / $17.95

Pearl Jam – Ten
00694882 / $14.95

Pink Floyd – Dark Side Of The Moon
00660172 / $14.95

Pink Floyd – Early Classics
00660119 / $14.95

The Best Of The Police
00660207 / $14.95

Queen – The Bass Collection
00690065 / $17.95

Rage Against the Machine
00690248 / $14.95

Red Hot Chili Peppers – Blood Sugar Sex Magik
00690064 / $17.95

Red Hot Chili Peppers – One Hot Minute
00690091 / $18.95

Best Of U2
00694783 / $18.95

Stevie Ray Vaughan – In Step
00694777 / $14.95

FOR MORE INFORMATION, SEE YOUR LOCAL MUSIC DEALER,
OR WRITE TO:

HAL•LEONARD® CORPORATION
7777 W. BLUEMOUND RD. P.O. BOX 13819 MILWAUKEE, WI 53213

Prices, contents & availability subject to change without notice.

Stevie Ray Vaughan – Lightnin' Blues 1983-1987
00694778 / $19.95

0498

BASS BUILDERS
SERIES

A series of technique book/audio packages created for the purposeful building and development of your chops. Each volume is written by an expert in that particular technique. And with the inclusion of audio – either CD or cassette – the added dimension of hearing exactly how to play particular grooves and techniques makes this truly like a private lesson. Books include notes and tab.

Bass Fitness—An Exercising Handbook
by Josquin des Pres
200 exercises designed to help increase your speed, improve your dexterity, develop accuracy and promote finger independence. Recommended by world-acclaimed bass players, music schools and music magazines!
00660177 Book Only...$7.95

Bass Improvisation—
The Complete Guide to Soloing
by Ed Friedland
CD includes over 50 tracks for demonstration and play-along. The book works for electric or acoustic bass and covers: modes, harmonic minor, melodic minor, blues, pentatonics, diminished, whole tone, Lydian b7, and other important scales; phrasing, chord/scale concepts, melodic development, using your ear; and much more.
00695164 Book/CD Pack $17.95

Building Walking Bass Lines
by Ed Friedland
A walking bass line is the most common approach to jazz bass playing, but it is also used in rock music, blues, rockabilly, R&B, gospel, latin, country and many other types of music. The specific goal of this book is to familiarize players with the techniques used to build walking bass lines and to make them aware of how the process works. Through the use of 90-minutes' worth of recorded rhythm tracks, players will have the opportunity to put the new learning directly into action.
00696503 Book/Cassette Pack...$12.95
00695008 Book/CD Pack $17.95

Expanding Walking Bass Lines
by Ed Friedland
A follow-up to *Building Walking Bass Lines*, this book approaches more advanced walking concepts, including model mapping, the two-feel, several "must know changes," and other important jazz bass lessons.
00695026 Book/CD Pack $19.95

Fingerboard Harmony For Bass
A Linear Approach For 4-, 5- and 6-String Bass
by Gary Willis
Learn the theory and geometry of the bass fingerboard from one of today's leading players and instructors. The CD features Gary Willis demonstrating 99 examples and exercises. This comprehensive book covers hand positions, key centers, the linear approach, and much more.
00695043 Book/CD Pack $17.95

Funk Bass
by Jon Liebman
Critically acclaimed as the best single source for the techniques used to play funk and slap-style bass! Includes a foreword by John Patitucci and is endorsed by Rich Appleman of the Berklee College Of Music, Will Lee, Mark Egan, Stuart Hamm and many others! Features several photos and a special section on equipment and effects. A book for everyone – from beginners to advanced players! Includes a 58-minute audio accompaniment.
00699347 Book/Cassette Pack...$14.95
00699348 Book/CD Pack $17.95

Funk/Fusion Bass
by Jon Liebman
This follow-up to *Funk Bass* studies the techniques and grooves of today's top funk/fusion bass players. It includes sections on mastering the two-finger technique, string crossing, style elements, establishing a groove, building a funk/fusion soloing vocabulary, and a CD with over 90 tracks to jam along with. Features a foreword written by Earth, Wind And Fire bassist Verdine White.
00696553 Book/CD Pack $19.95

Jazz Bass
by Ed Friedland
This book/CD pack features over 50 examples covering walking bass, the two feel, 3/4 time, Latin, and ballads. It covers soloing, performance protocol, and includes seven complete tunes.
00695084 Book/CD Pack $17.95

The Lost Art of Country Bass
An Inside Look at Country Bass for Electric and Upright Players
by Keith Rosiér
endorsed by Leland Sklar and Glenn Worf
This book/CD pack teaches classic and modern bass lines in the style of Hank Williams, Lefty Frizzell, Marty Stuart, David Ball, and others. You'll learn: what gear the pros use; how to be a studio bassist; how to read music with the Nashville Numbering System; and more. The CD includes 33 songs with full band backing. In standard notation and tab.
00695107 Book/CD Pack $17.95

Muted Grooves
by Josquin des Pres
Develop the string muting, string raking, and right-hand techniques used by the greatest legends of bass with this comprehensive exercise book. It includes over 100 practical exercises with audio accompaniments for each.
00696554 Book/Cassette Pack $12.95
00696555 Book/CD Pack $16.95

Simplified Sight-Reading for Bass
From the Fundamentals to the Entire Fingerboard
by Josquin des Pres
This book/CD pack helps bass players expand their reading skills. Beneficial for beginners through advanced players, this pack covers rhythms, notes, intervals, accidentals, and key signatures, as well as common bass patterns in blues, R&B, funk, rock, and more. The CD includes 97 demo tracks!
00695085 Book/CD Pack $17.95

Slap Bass Essentials
by Josquin des Pres and Bunny Brunel
This book/audio pack includes over 140 essential patterns and exercises covering every aspect of slap bass, written by two of today's hottest bass players Josquin des Pres and Bunny Brumell.
00696563 Book/CD Pack $16.95